# LOOKIN' BACK

Published by: A3TCO
PO Box 9181
Salem OR 97305

Cover Design and Artwork by Sheila Somerville. The artist may be contacted by writing to A3TCO.

This is a work of fiction. All the characters and events portrayed in this book are fictional, and any resemblance to real people or incidents is purely coincidental.

All rights reserved, including those of translation. This book, or parts thereof, may not be produced in any form without the written permission of the author. Neither the author, nor the publisher, by production of this material, ensure to anyone the use of such material against liability of any kind, including infringement of any patent.

Copyright 1995 - Gary D. Trump
Printed in the United States - Third Edition

ISBN: 1-884366-01-5

Other books in the Uncle Bud series:

I Remember When
Sweet Memories
Reflections
Yesterdays
What's Cookin'?

Hey! Glad to see you're back. When we heard you were coming, we took up a collection to get you a welcome back gift. We took the money down to the statehouse to buy you a politician, but they were sold out. Fortunately, there was enough in the fund to buy you a cup of coffee. Cream and sugar?

You should hear these old mossy horns come in here and complain every morning. Ornery old devils. I think I've come up with a solution though. Starting tomorrow, I'm gonna pull a switch and fill their coffee cups with hot prune juice.

Joe says that the only time he grabs for the gusto these days is when he loses his balance.

If friendship was money, a dog would open his wallet and give you all he had. A cat might possibly offer you a contract after he'd audited your books.

You see that old rattletrap pickup passin' by? That's Frank McCalister. He has a big ranch about forty miles out. Frank runs sheep and cattle. One spring he had a fella come walkin' up to his house. The guy says, "Lookin' for a job."

"Well," says Frank, "I got a job open for a man to herd sheep up in the mountains. You'd be livin' in a little trailer by yourself with nobody to talk to for six months except three dogs and a couple thousand sheep."

The fellow looks Frank over a while and says, "Okay."

Six months later when they brought the sheep back, Frank wrote the herder a check and said "How'd it go?".

"Trailer roof leaks," the fellow said, and took his pay and left.

The next spring the man showed up one morning, nodded to Frank and took the herd back to the mountains. That fall Frank wrote him a check and said, "How'd it go?".

"Roof still leaks," the herder said, and left.

In the spring the fella was back again, nodded to Frank again and took the herd back into the mountains. That fall Frank handed him his check and said "How'd it go?".

"Roof still leaks. I quit," the herder replied.

"Good," said Frank. "If you're gonna be whinin' and complainin' all the time, I'm glad to be rid of you."


The one great advantage of fools is that they never lose arguments.

I know what a lot of folks are saying about the economy and the country in general these days. I guess I just have one question. If business doesn't work -- who does?


Dad always rolled his own cigarettes, and he bought his tobacco in those big old five pound cans. As kids, we kept a close eye on the operation. It told us how things were goin'.

When Dad rolled his cigarettes so big and fat that the edges of the paper just barely overlapped, then things were on the rise. Times were good and we were doin' well. But when those cigarettes got so small and skinny that they were more paper than tobacco -- look out below!


Sometimes it's good to keep in mind that when the tigers get hungry, they find liberals and conservatives equally tasty.


"What's your lunch special today?" Joe asked.

"Fried chicken," I replied.

"Boy, I do love fried chicken," Luther put in, "but I don't like the breast. Too dry. I like legs and thighs, just like my Uncle Rufus. That's what killed him in the end."

"Too much fried chicken plugs up your pipes," nodded Tom.

"Wasn't that," Luther sighed. "Uncle Rufus raised chickens."

Pete's eyes narrowed as he looked over the rim of his cup. "Eggs or meat?" he asked, as he lowered his brew to the table.

"Eggs."

"So," Pete said, with a tight little smile, "pickin' cackleberries killed your Uncle Rufus."

"No, no," Luther shook his head. "Uncle Rufus loved chicken legs fried up nice and brown. He was a young man and had just started his chicken farm when he noticed one of his roosters had his wings set kind of low down. It gave Uncle Rufus an idea, and he went to work breeding that rooster to certain hens. After forty years of work and Lord knows how many generations of chickens, he finally had what he went after -- a four legged chicken."

"A four legged chicken," Pete nodded. "Two extra legs per bird. I'll bet they tasted so good your uncle ate 'em all up."

"Nope," Luther said, sadly. "That's what killed him. The old feller died of a broken heart. Them chickens was so damn fast he never could catch one to find out."


It is said among professions law is the second oldest. Maybe. I keep confusing it with the first.

4

Doctor: "You may feel a little discomfort."
Lawyer: "There will be a nominal fee."
Translation: "This is gonna hurt like hell."


Doc Guthrie stops in for coffee with us once in a while when she has time. She started out as an Army nurse and spent time caring for combat casualties in a field hospital. Later on she went back to school and became a doctor. It wasn't an easy thing to do back then, but as she likes to say, "I'm a tough ol' heifer." She is, too, and she's been lookin' out for folks around here for years.

I put off goin' to her for a long time, but after Doc Krebbs died, I finally gave in. I'm glad I did. Doc Krebbs was always railin' on about how folks should get lots of exercise, eat right, not drink or smoke, until it got pretty tiresome. Of course, he lived up to all his recommendations right up until the day he dropped dead at age forty-six.

Now, Doc Guthrie feels the same way as Doc Krebbs did, but she doesn't get on her high horse about it. As a matter of fact, if you should have her over for supper, when the meal's finished, she ain't goin' to turn down a snifter of brandy and a good see-gar.


Glass coffee pot stained? Add an ice cube and a little water, swish it around. Takes out the stains.

Martha bought one of those talking bathroom scales a while back, but it only works half the time. She stands on it and it tells her what she weighs. I get on it and it says, "One at a time, please."


Alice, Tom's wife, was in having coffee with us the other day and made a comment about sitting with five handsome men.

Tom couldn't stand it, and mentioned that Pete's nose was big enough that if a fella was to lift it up, he could reasonably expect to find an engine under it. Luther, he said, had ears that made him look like a Hudson headin' down the road with the suicide doors open, while Joe was a dead ringer, he claimed, for Adolf Hitler. Not wanting to leave anyone out, he thought I was probably Tomaine Mary in a former life and complained that the reason I opened a cafe was to feed him slow poison by cooking six days out of seven.

Alice just sat there and grinned through the whole thing, defending each of us in turn. Well, Tom is bald, and the remarks started flyin' back and forth about being blinded by the reflection and how he should be wearing a net around his ears because the flies that land on his head keep skiddin' off and crashin' to their deaths.

Tom's head was "ballistically correct," Pete said, and now he's been nicknamed "ol' bullet head."

And so he will remain until we've decided honor is satisfied.

Funny, we get along just fine. But, ahhh, the ladies, God bless 'em, when they really decide they want to dip their oar in and muddy up the water, they can sit back and watch the fur fly while we men make dopes of ourselves.


"I'm not bald," Tom maintains. "I just have a wider part in my hair than most fellas."


I once put my arm around Martha and said, "Sweetheart, if the world is a chocolate sundae, you're the cherry on top."

Patting me on the cheek, she smiled and replied, "Thank you, dear. And you're one of the nuts."


If you still buy your oranges in plastic mesh bags, be sure to save the bag. They're good scrubbers for big pots and pans and work well on whitewall tires. We used to unwrap all our bar soap and hang it in one of these bags. Soap that's had a chance to dry out lasts longer. Now we just put it in a hanging basket in the bathroom.

Fools are easier to spot against a background of money.


I'm a traditionalist. I believe in giving kids and dogs good ol' tried and true names. Curt, Kyle, Cathy, Karen, Tip, Shep; they're all names that are easy to yell, for the simple reason that you can never find a kid or a dog when you want 'em.


We'd all just sat down the other morning when Joe lifted his cup and said, "They say drinkin' coffee makes you look older."

"I'd have to agree with that," nodded Pete. "I've been drinkin' it for around fifty years now and, by golly, I do look older."


"You know," Luther says, " when I bought my farm, I got it from a feller who'd let the place go to wrack an' ruin. I saw the FOR SALE sign and pulled in. This old guy was settin' on the porch of a house that you wouldn't keep chickens in -- it was a real wreck. There was a mangy old dog barkin' at me when I drove up. I rolled down the pickup window and hollered up at this feller."

*Does your dog bite?*

*Nope*, the feller says.

"I get out and the mutt takes a hunk out of my

laig," Luther says indignantly. "I yelled at the guy while I pulled a shovel out of the back to defend myself."

*I thought you said your dog don't bite?*

*Ain't my dog*, the feller says.

Luther takes a sip of coffee. "Well," he says, "in those days the farm was quite a distance from anywhere's else. The city and the suburbs have grown a lot closer now than they used to be. It was quite a hike to town back then.

"Anyhow, the feller that owned the place, Phipps his name was, he showed me around. The inside of the house was torn all apart. What happened? I asked.

*Well*, Phipps says, *I go to town ever' once in a while. The past few months when I'd go to town, some low down skunk would come by the house and make free.*

*How's that?* I asked.

*Well*, Phipps goes on, *they'd come in and light a fire in the stove, cook up my grub and eat. Then they'd leave. Wouldn't split no kindlin'. Left the dirty dishes for me to wash. I don't mind somebody fixin' himself somethin' to eat if I'm not around, but by damn, they'd better refill the wood box and wash the dishes!* His lip curled up and you could tell he was real disgusted. *I hate that*, he said. *I just hate it.*

*I take it*, I said with another look around at the sad state of things, *that this has somethin' to do with what I see here.*

*I'd had enough*, Phipps said. *That old stove had a crack in the firebox. I tied up three or four sticks of dynamite, capped a fuse and put it all in the oven. From there I could run that fuse through the crack and up into the firebox. After I done that, I filled the firebox with kindlin' an' I went to town. I'd had enough*, he repeated.

*And then?* I asked.

*I had a lot to do in town*, Phipps said. *It was real late when I got home, and I hadn't had no supper. I plumb forgot about the dynamite. I lit a fire in the stove.*

*And?* I said.

*Blowed me right outta my socks*, Phipps replied. *If you look at the underside of that old oak table, you'll see it's full of scrap iron. That's what saved me. I wound up out there in the yard with nothin' on but my overhauls. I give it a lotta thought since then*, he said, *an' I conclude that the no-account trespasser that was doin' me dirt was here, all right. He looked in the oven before he lit the stove an' he left that dynamite there on purpose.* He frowned and scratched an ear. *It's one thing to know you've got a neighbor is ornery an' inconsiderate*, he said, *but when they start tryin' to kill you, it's time to move out.*

"That reminds me of the time I was travelin' down south," said Joe. "I was in the Navy at the time

11

and drivin' to my new base. Well, the day was hot, the road was hotter, my ol' car was about to boil and I was gettin' medium rare. Along out there amongst the vines and brush, I come on this pretty little lake. An old fella was sittin' out there in a boat fishin' and smokin' a corncob pipe.

"I pulled over, got out and walked down to the shore. While I was strippin' down to my skivvies, this old timer just sat in his boat puffin' his pipe and watchin' his bobber.

"I was a young smart aleck at the time and figgered what I didn't know wasn't worth knowin', but just before I dived into the water, I got to thinkin' that this country was new to me and had critters a fella didn't see where I come from.

*Hey! Old man!* I yelled. He just sat there.
*Hey, old man! You deaf?* I hollered.
*Ain't deef,* he finally said.
*There any cottonmouths in this lake?*
*Nope,* he says.
*Water moccasins?*
*Nope!*
*Any kind of snake?*
*Ain't no kind of snake, pizen er otherwise in this here lake,* the old feller says.

"Well, I dove in and, man, that water felt good. I paddled around a while and finally swam about halfway out to the old guy. I was treadin' water and the old feller was watchin' me real close. You know how some ol' devil will stand an' watch you walk into his yard when he's got a mean dog? That kind of look.

*Hey, old man,* I said, feelin' a mite odd. *How come there ain't no snakes in this lake?*

"The old geezer took his time. He dug out a match, struck it on a button of his bib overalls and held it to his pipe. He kept starin' at me while he puffed his pipe back to life, and then smiled at me as he flipped the match in into the water.

*The gators ate 'em.*

"You know, you can't win," Pete was saying this morning. "When things are going bad, your ego hurts and when things are going good, your conscience does.

Strange how some politicians demanded an air bag in every new car. Well, any car with a politician inside already has one.

When our son Curt was, oh, maybe eight or nine, he took up swearin'. We tried to break him of it, but every once in a while he'd cut loose with a few choice cuss words. Martha finally told him that we never used that kind of language in our house (okay, so I slip once in a while), and the next time he started cussin', she was gonna throw him out of the house.

The next evening, as I was pulling into the driveway, there was Curt, toting a little suitcase and heading for the road. I stopped and rolled down the window.

"Leavin', huh?" I asked.

"Yep," said Curt. "Guess so."

I saw the curtains move at the living room window, so I knew Martha was watching us. I turned back to Curt. "What happened, Mom catch you cussin' again?"

"Yep," Curt nodded. "Packed my suitcase and threw me out. I been standin' out here tryin' to figger out where I'm gonna go."

I kept my face straight and slowly nodded my head. "Well, that's sure too bad," I said, playin' along with Martha's game.

I was about to tell Curt that if he'd promise to stop cussin', I'd talk to Mom and see if maybe she'd let him come back home. Still, Curt was dry-eyed and, even though he looked pretty solemn, he didn't seem particularly scared. I decided to make him squirm just a little.

"Well, Curt," I said, "we'll sure miss you around here. Where you headed now?"

Curt put down his suitcase and folded his arms across his chest. He frowned and pulled his mouth to one side as he thought about it. Finally, he looked up at me and spoke.

"I'll be damned if I know."

15

Some things never change. For example, the departing guest who takes twenty minutes to say "goodbye" while holding your door open in summer and letting the flies in is the same dolt who holds it open in the winter when it's ten below zero.

You have to be careful of a man who says he's the boss at his house. He probably lies about other things, too.

Hell was probably a much more pleasant place before all the lawyers moved in.

There was a fella named Burly Grimes who owned a piece of land on the river. Once Burly announced he was gonna build himself a houseboat. Now, Burly wasn't especially handy with tools, and some of the neighbors got to kiddin' ol' Burly that he might get it built, but he'd never make it waterproof. They all told him the thing would sink as soon as it was launched.

Well, Burly just shook his head and went to work. He monkeyed with that thing off and on for maybe three years. He took special care with the hull. Most folks admitted he'd done a fine job. Not to his face, of course. When Burly was in earshot, all they could talk about was how that boat would most likely sink like a stone.

There was a pond on Burly's place that was maybe forty feet across and a foot deep during the rainy season. The rest of the time it was mostly just mud. All of a sudden the word went around that, instead of launching his houseboat in the river, Burly had winched it out onto that pond. We went out for a look. Sure enough, there it sat, lacking maybe ten feet of stretching from shore to shore.

"Burly," folks were askin', "why'd you do that? There isn't even enough water for it to float."

"That may be," Burly replied, "but, by gum, it didn't sink, neither."

Well, time went by and the boat settled into the mud to where Burly's winch and a half dozen skyhooks weren't gonna move the thing. Burly spent some time on the boat alright, but eventually it settled at an angle. Then one night it caught fire and burned to the water (mud) line.

For a long time around these parts, the term "launchin' your boat in Burly's pond" was another way of sayin' "playing it safe." It was quite a lesson to a kid like me.

I grew up tellin' myself, *When I build my ship, I'm not launchin' it in Burly's pond. I'm goin' where the water's deep.*


A basic part of the "new philosophy" in the country is to eliminate the old prejudices. Well, they seem to be gettin' it done alright, but I get the feeling that they're doin' it by replacing them with their own.

Martha joined a group of local women who welcome newcomers to the community. They're always on the scout for somebody movin' in. I told her they're going at it the wrong way. All they have to do is stand around the cash register at the grocery store. When they spot somebody buyin' zuchinni, it's a sure bet they don't know anybody for miles around.

Young Dennis Coe comes in for breakfast every morning. The other day he got here before I opened (officially), and he sat down with the rest of us for coffee. Now, in Dennis' defense, he had just started a new job and had a new girlfriend. He likes 'em both.

Anyhow, Dennis was about to bust his buttons over it all and just couldn't help lettin' everybody know how he felt.

"It's a wonderful world," he said with a big grin. "A perfect world. Things couldn't be any better."

After he left, Luther shook his head and smiled. "I'm afraid he's wrong."

"Wrong?" Pete muttered. "Hell, I'm not afraid he's wrong. I'm afraid he might be right."

Oh sure, I go to the city once in a while, but I'm happy to live in this little one-horse town. Cities always seemed to me to be places where folks spend what they don't have, buying what they don't need, to impress people they don't like.

A lot of times country folks see things a little differently than city folks. Once, when I was a kid, my aunt brought a lady from the city out to see the folks. She was a nice enough lady, I guess, and she really fell in love with the place. Pretty soon, Lenore, that was her name, took to coming out alone. Not long after that, she started bringing her friends along.

Now, it's not that country folks are antisocial - far from it - but they do have to make a livin', and so they can't always stop to entertain people who make a habit of stoppin' by. Lenore seemed a little put out by it, but she'd been around enough by then that she could show her lady friends around without our help. She seemed to take to it real well, and by the time she'd given three or four guided tours, I was beginning to get the feeling that she only let us stay on because she needed somebody to watch the place while she was gone.

At one point one of those ladies asked Dad if his title was "manager or foreman." Dad let it slide until one day Lenore and her crowd showed up while he was workin' in the barn.

Dad was puttin' new rivets in some harness, as I recall, when Lenore herded her group in the door. He just nodded when they came in and kept on workin'. After a while, the ladies got tired of gettin' into things and found themselves at the big back door that was standing open. There was a small pasture out there and a single steer munchin' the grass that came up to his knees. Dad, like he did every fall, had picked out a steer to fatten up for our winter's meat.

"Why is that cow out there all by itself?" one of the ladies asked.

"Well," Lenore replied, "that cow is something of a pet around here. I call her Lucy." She turned to Dad. "Isn't that right, Spence?"

Dad pulled a sack of tobacco out of his shirt pocket and began to roll a smoke. "Can't say we've got any pets on the place," he said. "And I just call him a steer."

"Then why is he there?" another lady asked.

"Well," Dad replied, as he licked the cigarette paper, "that's so I can grain him ... get him fat enough to butcher."

"What?" Lenore almost yelled. "How can you do that? How can you raise them and then ... ughh," she shuddered, "kill them?"

"I don't look at it that way," Dad said, as he pulled out a match and struck it with his thumbnail. "Me an' this steer have an agreement."

"What kind of agreement?" Lenore demanded.

Dad put the match to his cigarette and squinted through the smoke. "I feed him a while ... he feeds me a while."

Sometimes I wonder whatever happened to Lenore.


"One thing we can take comfort in with our morning coffee sessions," Tom was saying a while back. "There hasn't been one thing said that's so stupid or foolish or just plain ol' dumb that some college professor hasn't said it before."


The best students usually make the worst teachers.


Herman Snipes was about the most ornery tight-fisted old devil in the country. Granted, there are a few around today who could give him a run for his money, but most folks agree that Herman established the benchmark for all the rest. We were talking about him just the other day.

"When our youngest boy, Jason, was about ten or eleven," said Pete, "he had a new teacher in school. She thought, what with all the farmers and ranchers around here, she could use the local economy to make arithmetic more interesting.

"School was just gettin' started good that fall

when she gave it a try. *Class,* she says, *Mr. Snipes raises hay which he is offering for sale at twenty dollars per ton.* (Which was true enough.) *Your father gives Mr. Snipes one hundred dollars for hay. How many tons of hay does your father receive from Mr. Snipes?*

"Well, Jason grabs his pencil and gets to work. Pretty soon he raises his hand."

*Jason?* the teacher says.

*I make it out to be about four and three quarter ton,* Jason replies.

*Hmmm,* says the teacher. *It is obvious you haven't a good grasp of mathematics.*

*No,* Jason snaps back. *It's obvious you ain't never bought hay from Herman Snipes!*


When I was a kid, the folks in town got together and built a community hall. It was used for various events with the proceeds going to the volunteer fire department and such. At one point, somebody came up with the idea of holding a dance every Saturday night to raise more money.

It seemed like a good idea at first, but then some odd looking characters started turning up. You know, those guys who don't have hair on the backs of their fingers because they're always draggin' 'em on the ground? Some of those louts were pretty big, too. One of 'em had a bathing beauty tattooed on his back -- actual size. There got to be more of 'em every week. Some of 'em even tried to dance, but that just looked like racing silks on a jackass. All they were really there for was to drink and fight.

One fella drove quite a distance to bring his wife to the dance. He telephoned the next week to say it was the only place he'd ever been that he had to fight his way in and then fight his way out. The city fathers got the message and closed down the dance.

There was one problem though. The idiots who caused all the trouble showed up for two more weekends of drinkin' and fightin' before they figured out the place was locked up.


Pete claims that his kids were always ornery little varmints. "I tried to teach 'em to be polite and honest, use good manners, be neat and clean ..." he says with a shake of his head. "It never worked. The little monsters insisted on actin' like me."


Martha uses a blow dryer quite a lot. It took a while for us to figure out that the intake screen on the dryer gets plugged with lint over time and makes the thing overheat and burn out. We use the hose on the vacuum to clean it out every few months.


Luther is a real fashion plate. He insists that

the legs on his overalls should just touch the laces on his work boots.

Ever notice that parents think heredity is so much baloney while grandparents think it never misses?

So you've got a yardful of moles and gophers? Well, I've tried most of the things that are rumored to work from the slightly oddball to the downright daffy. The best thing I've found for moles is a trap or one of the commercial poisons put out for that purpose. But gophers? Okay, maybe it is daffy, but chewing gum works on the ones around here. Not just any chewing gum, now. It has to be the right kind. How can I describe this stuff without getting a manufacturer mad? Hey, would you want people to know your chewing gum kills gophers? Not that there's anything wrong with the gum, of course. What do you think the effect would be (considering the difference in size between you and a gopher) if you ate, say, five pounds of chewing gum? Right. You could mark trips to the bathroom off your schedule for the rest of your life, limited though it might be.

When I find a gopher mound in my yard, I scrape it away and dig out the hole. I unwrap the gum, being careful not to touch it and leave my scent

on the stuff.  Okay, maybe it doesn't matter, but what can it hurt?  Anyhow, I place two sticks well down in the hole.  I've got a tree with large leaves, so I use one to cover the hole and then cover that with dirt.  If you don't have large leaves handy, a piece of paper should do the same thing.  The idea is to block out the light without covering up the gum.  In a couple of days, I open the hole again to see if the gopher will stop it up again.  They rarely do.

I've only found one kind of gum that works.  What kind?  Well, let's just say it has to be juicy ... and fruity ... and in a yellow wrapper.


A few good salesmen and every kid knows that the more often people say no, the more likely they are to say yes.


Okay.  Let's all just admit it.  I've got a junk drawer in the kitchen and so do you.  Everybody has one, and although they may stick a high-falutin' name on it, it's still a junk drawer.

There are things in that junk drawer that I can't identify.  Most of 'em are parts to stuff we had at one time or another and wound up in that drawer.  I can't really get rid of them, though, because as soon as I do, something in the house will break down and I'll realize the part I need is that thing I threw away last week.

I took a close look at ours the other day. There was tape, curtain hooks, rubber bands, string, and a few tools. There was also a raggedly old deck of cards, a couple of dried out tubes of glue, an old flashlight battery that hasn't had a charge since the Eisenhower administration -- and keys.

Let me tell you about keys. There are keys in there that fit DeSotos and Studebakers. There are keys to padlocks that were melted down for scrap twenty years ago and made into new padlocks. There are keys that might fit suitcases that are so old and raggedy and beat up, the lock is the only thing that still works. I keep saying I'm going to haul those old wrecks down out of the attic some day and throw 'em away ... but we can't get rid of the keys because one or two (out of a dozen or so) probably fits one of those old suitcases.

Oh, yeah, I almost forgot. Back there in a corner of the drawer is a padlock. Nice padlock, too. It's a shame there isn't a single damn key in the drawer that fits it.


Many years ago a slipshod farm or ranch operation often was called a "rawhide" outfit due to the owner's habit of using rawhide to tie up, patch up or hold together anything that needed it. Later on, people started baling hay instead of puttin' it up loose. Ah, haywire. If it wasn't for haywire, half the country would have gone to wrack and ruin. A haywire outfit came to mean the same as the rawhide variety, and it isn't hard to figure out how the term" it went haywire" came about.

Everybody used haywire, some for temporary repairs and others because they were too poor, too lazy, or too cheap to use anything else. One fella, old Ernie Kern, had more money than he knew what to do with, and he got it 'cause he was tighter'n the bark on a willer tree. For a long time around our neck of the woods, haywire was known as Ernie Kern bolts.


Luther says he watches politics for the same reason a lot of folks watch car races. He ain't so interested in who wins as in who has to be scraped off the track.


Having a kid or a wasp in the house is about the same. The damage usually isn't done until the noise stops.


"When I was a young man I pert near never lost an argument," Pete was sayin' a while back.

"Oh, I'll bet," Joe laughed.

"No, it's true," Pete went on. "For example, one time I hauled a load of feeder steers to the sale yard. You may not remember ol' Dudley

Spurlock, but he ran the yard there for several years. He always dressed western, Ol' Dudley did, gray western cut suit, white hat and fancy white shirt, string tie, the whole shootin' match. Had him a gold an' silver belt buckle that looked like the steerin' wheel off a DeSoto."

"Anyhow, I had hauled them calves to the auction and instead of goin' home like I usually did, I hung around til they sold. Ol' Dudley was gettin' a reputation for not bein' any more honest than he had to be, so I wasn't gonna let him mail me a check and maybe squeeze out a little more commission than he had comin'.

"The tote board, as I recall, showed those calves to weigh out to a total of 5,300 pounds. I waited til the sale was about over and went around to pick up the check. They paid me for 5,100 pounds of beef.

*This ain't right*, I says to the clerk.

*It's what the scale man gave me*, she says.

"Well, I'd been standin' there watchin' the whole time, and ol' Dudley had been spellin' off the scale man when my stock went through. I looked around and there stands the scale man drinkin' a cup of coffee. I knew right where to find my man. Dudley was fiddlin' with the balance beam, weighin' out a bunch of sheep when I got there.

*You made a mistake on my calves*, I said.

"Dudley looked around and did a double take. *What're you ... we don't make mistakes*, he says.

*You did this time,* I says.

*I'm busy,* Dudley mutters. *You go on home.
I'll look into it. If there's a mistake, I'll send you a
check.*

*There has been a mistake. You will fix it.
And you'll do it right now.*

*Get out of here!*

"Now Dudley was tall and thin with long,
white hands that had never seen a blister, let alone a
callus. The last horse he ever throwed a leg over was
of the hobby variety. Hell, your old Aunt Nellie
could whip him. But I had the feelin' that whippin'
him wasn't gonna get me my money.

"Dudley kind of shot his sleeves out from his
suit coat like some fellers do and flicked an
imaginary speck of dust from his cuff. *Get out of
here before I call the cops!*

"I reached into my back pocket and pulled out
my tobacco pouch. Dudley was pretendin' not to
notice me while I dug out a wad about half the size
of a baseball and stuffed it in my left cheek. *Listen,
Dud,* I says, *just pay me what you owe me, and I'll
walk right out of here.* I was lettin' my voice raise,
not yellin' yet, but not bein' quiet, either.

*I told you that ...*

"He was watchin' me dig out another wad  and
stuff it in my right cheek.  I looked like a squirrel
packin' around his whole winters' groceries.

*You get out of here right ...*

"The trick is to buy chewin' tobacco that's

30

been treated with honey or sugar. It makes your mouth water somethin' fierce, and when you're really loaded up, it wants to trickle out the corners of your mouth and drip off your chin like I was lettin' it do right then. Dudley was starin' at me, and his face had gone all pasty lookin'.

*Phhhhive thousand one hundred pounds ain't right!* I yelled.

"Dud jumped back, touched his pinky to his face and then looked at it real disgusted like. There was a gate onto the scale and Dud backed through it with me right behind him. The sheep was runnin' around blattin' their heads off, and while Dud was backin' away and watchin' me, he got all kinds of nasty stuff all over those shiny, expensive boots.

*Dud,* I hollered, *I been haulin' phhhive or ten head of calphhhs in here ephhhry phhriday phhhor pert near phhhive years ...*

"Dud threw open the gate and backed into the sale ring where ever'body could not only hear us, they could see us, too.

*... and ephhher since you took ophher, I get the phheelin' I'm bein' phhlim-phhhlammed.*

"Dud's shirt and suit was startin' to look kind of speckled. So was his face and hat. By the time I'd backed him across the sale ring, he looked like a big ol' pinto bean.

*Please,* he was sayin', *Don't! Oh, Lord! Get away from me! I think I'm gonna be sick. Ugh! This is ... ugh! Really disgusting. Oh, Lord!*

"I took a deep breath."

*NO!* Dud yelled. *How much! How much do you think they weighed?*

*Phhi-phhty phhive hundred,* I bellered.

"Dud wiped his eyes with a single finger of each hand and looked up at the clerk who was takin' all this in. *Write it up,* he said."

Pete took a sip of coffee and sat back. "I never lost an argument in them days," he smiled. "And if you clowns don't straighten up, I won't again."


Have you noticed that kids always wait to start their latest growing stage until just after you've bought all their new school clothes?


I like to talk to folks. I like to find out who they are, what they do for a living, that kind of thing. You sure can meet some interesting people if you take the time to get to know them a little bit. I talk to folks here at the cafe, in line at the market or the bank, and, especially in the waiting room at the doctor's office. That's because at the doctor's office I usually have a lot of extra time on my hands. I've met all kinds of people there ... people in just about every job and profession you can think of ... except one. The only person I've never met in a doctor's waiting room is a doctor.

Lawyers are never really buried. Once rigor mortis sets in, the guys at the cemetery just screw 'em into the ground.


Tom and Alice have a dog they call Winston. Now, Winston is about the size of a greyhound ... bus, and he's got enough hair so that when he's on the move, he looks like a walkin' haystack. Early every summer they go to cuttin' hair until they get down to dog. Last year Alice got the idea of makin' clothes out of ol' Winston's winter woolies. She spent a small fortune, so Tom claims, on spinnin' wheels and whatnot and finally came up with two or three bucks worth of yarn.

They go for walks every evening, so Alice made Tom a pair of leg warmers. Now if you've never seen leg warmers, they're kind of economically disadvantaged pants from the knees up and a misfitted sweater from the knees down.

Alice came in a few days ago with Tom hobbling along behind, and they sat down with the rest of us. "It was those stupid leg warmers Alice made me wear," he claimed. "We were walkin' down the street mindin' our own business and, I'll have to admit, my bum knee was feeling pretty good. Then a cat ambled out in front of us and the next thing I knew I'd cut across two lanes of traffic, passed a kid on a motor scooter and veered back across in front of a loggin' truck. I'd almost caught that cat when we came to a fire hydrant. That's when I threw my hip out of joint."

"Oh, baloney!" snorted Alice. "He slipped on some ice."

"Yeah, well," Tom grumbled, "it would heal faster if I could just keep myself from chasin' cars."

"True," Alice shot back, "but I'm throwing you out of the house the next time I catch you drinking out of the toilet."

There are several outfits making this rubber preservative stuff. They make all kinds of suggestions about using it, but they forgot to mention windshield wipers. Mine last at least twice as long when I use this stuff on 'em.

Some folks think of themselves as straight-forward and forthright when they're really just rude.

You may recall we talked about Herman Snipes awhile back. Ol' Herman and his wife lived a couple miles out of town. They didn't associate with folks much ... or maybe it was the other way around. Herman 'n Hattie were both ornery enough to curdle cream.

You would see them a few times a year drivin' their old Model A into town to do some shopping.

They didn't buy much in the way of groceries, though. Just the basics. That's all they needed, because any critter unlucky enough to wander onto their place stood a good chance of winding up in the pot. Well, after they'd hung it on the clothesline to "season" for a few days. Mostly they ate ducks and muskrats.

That sounds a little rough I know, but to top it off, Hattie was the daughter of one of the pioneers of this country and had inherited a fortune. When she married Herman, he already owned the place they were to live, and it amounted to about 1300 acres. Their attitude was that it ain't how much you make ... it's how much you don't spend.

Anyhow, there was a young fella workin' for Jake Barker, who owned the place next to Herman's. This kid liked to rip around on a motorcycle, drivin' like a maniac. Workin' for Jake, he knew all about Herman.

"I'd only been here a few months," Doc Guthrie was sayin', "and I was driving back from visiting a patient when I happened on an accident. Herman had been driving a mule and wagon across the road when this young man came around the curve, going too fast, as usual, and ran into the mule, breaking its leg. Herman, it seems had just shot the mule dead without even getting out of the wagon. Now, I'd been called out to see Hattie once, and I knew that mule. He was old, gray, mean and one-eyed, just like Herman. The only real difference between them was that Herman wore an eyepatch. Anyway, the mule was dead, the motorcycle was on its side, and the kid was sitting on the shoulder of the road. I stopped to see if anyone was hurt.

"The kid just glanced at me and then stared up at Herman. *I'm fine, Doc. Never better. Everything's fine. May as well be on your way. We're all fine here.*

"Well, there wasn't much I could do, it seemed, so I got back in my car and came on to town. Half an hour later, the kid was in my office. He had cuts and scrapes, a sprained wrist, and I had to pick gravel out of the skin around his knee. When I was done, I looked at the kid and said, *you told me you were alright.*"

*Listen,* the kid says, *I came around the curve and hit the mule. Herman looks him over and then pulls out his rifle and shoots him dead. Just as you drive up, he looks over at me and says, "You ain't hurt are ya?"*


Somebody who won't read isn't any better off than somebody who can't.


"I gotta tell you," says Luther, "where I went to high school, we had a girl in our class named "NO" Johnson. Well, NO wasn't her real name, of course, but ever'body, all the boys at least, called her

37

NO. Now you might think that the few times one of us fellers managed to get her into the rumble seat that NO was the word we heard most often, and that's sure enough true alright, but that's not how she got her name.

"Back in those days most folks still had the old wood ranges and the Johnson family had one made by the Vermont Stove Works. Like most stoves back then, it had the name cast on or riveted right across the front. The story was that when NO was ten or twelve years old she was taking a bath one cold winter's night in a tin tub next to the stove. Her mother had the old range stoked up good and hot, prob'ly heatin' more water and keepin' the house warm and whatnot. Anyhow, NO stood up to dry off and when she bent over she branded herself right on the ... uhh ... oh, hell, right on the butt. The rumor was that she had an "o" and an "n" from "Vermont" stamped on one cheek. Of course, that came out NO with the "N" being backwards. All the boys was just in a lather tryin' to find out if it was true.

"The one who was most curious was a guy named Harvey Granger and he did ever'thing he could think of and then some. Harvey was workin' under a handicap, though, 'cause NO didn't have any brothers to spill the beans. Her sisters all acted scandalized when the subject was brought up, so that was no help. Takin' NO on a date did no good, 'cause she lived up to her name. She was a pretty girl, too, and we all dated her at one time or another,

but always with the same result ... NO!

"I can't speak for the other fellers, but I have to admit I didn't try real hard. Her father was about the size of a milk wagon, horse included, and thought teenage boys were all apprentice thieves and murderers and should be done away with pronto before they could cause problems for decent folks like him and his family of daughters.

"The upshot of it all was that even though we all tried, none of us ever found out for certain. Oh sure, somebody would claim to have seen NO's brand once in a while, but it always turned out to be a lie. Harvey got kicked out of school for three days once when he was found hangin' from a limb next to a window of the girls' restroom. He claimed he was caught just as he was about to find out for sure, and I guess that's true enough, 'cause NO didn't speak to him again for over a year.

"School went on, time passed, and eventually so did we. I didn't see any of those kids until I went back for a ten year reunion. By golly, Harvey and NO were married. Harvey was workin' at the mill, and they had themselves a home, mortgage, car payments and two or three house apes.

"We got to talkin' about old times. Finally I said, "Harvey, you know I'd never ask a man anything personal about his wife, but the question I have in mind is one that we were all thinkin' about long before you and NO got hitched."

*Well*, he said, *it is personal*.

"I know," I told him, "and I ain't askin' for a detailed description or nothing.  I just want to know."
*Know what?*
"Has NO really got it branded on her ... uhh ... butt?
"Harvey just stood there and looked at me.
"Just tell me ... well ... what's there.
"Harvey grinned at me. *No,* he said, and walked away."


When it comes to when to say "who" and when to say "whom", I never seem to get it straight. Well, owls are supposed to be wise and you don't see them goin' around sayin' "Whom? Whom?"?


"I went to a wedding a while back," says Tom, "and there was some guy there wearing white tennis shoes. I couldn't believe it.  Some people have no class at all. Everybody knows that for formal occasions, any color of tennis shoe, other than black of course, is unacceptable."


When the kids were little, Martha used to put on birthday parties for them. There was one I recall that got so messy we wound up using all our old sheets for drop cloths. When it was finally over, Martha collapsed in a chair and said, "I swear the next birthday party is going to be held in the garage. That way, when it's over, we can just hose the place down."

"No," I replied. "We'll have the next party out in the old shed. That way, when it's over, we can just burn the place down."


Joe says he can't stand people with big egos. "They spend so much time talkin' about themselves," he says, "they never notice what a great guy I am."


"My mother," says Alice Bennet, "was a typical woman of her time and place. The cellar was always stocked with her home-canned fruits and vegetables. She was a good cook and baker and folks said she could cure ham and bacon as good as anybody. She made her own clothes, most of Dad's, and all of ours.

"Back in the days when Mom and Dad were starting married life together, practically every little town had its own flour mill. A lot of them sold their flour in sacks made of printed material. You bought your flour, took it home and dumped it in the bin and the sack, after it was washed, could be used for shirts or dresses or whatever might be needed.

"Mom always bought Carlson's Flour. It had their name printed at the top of the sack and their slogan at the bottom. There wasn't any bottom seam on their sacks, so you just took out the side seams of the sack, and you had a long strip of cloth. Not long after the folks were married, Mom decided she needed a new pair of drawers, and she used a Carlson's Flour sack to make them.

"Mother turned the material upside down on the pattern, cut it out and worked a good while getting her new drawers sewed together. She had just finished when Dad stopped by the house. *You've got to see what I made, dear,* she said. She rushed into the bedroom, took off her dress and underthings and pulled on her new drawers. *Come look, dear.*

"Dad stepped into the room and watched as she held out her arms and slowly did a complete turn. *Well, he said,* with an eyebrow raised, *is this a comment on our marriage or are you thinkin' about goin' to work to supplement our income?*

Mother wisted around and looked behind her. Printed across the seat of her new drawers was Carlson's slogan:

"THE BEST THAT MONEY CAN BUY."


It's nice to have grandma's old cut glassware and grandpa's silver inlaid fountain pen, and they might be valuable, too. But the old bread pans and cast iron cookware, the worn ax and shovel and battered old canteen -- that's where the real memories are. The fond, warm thoughts of people who cared enough about you to work hard and do things right.

The old wood range was the center of home life not so many years ago. It not only cooked the meals, but it heated the water for washing clothes and the flat irons to press them. It provided hot bricks for the foot of a cold bed on winter nights while it kept the kitchen toasty warm. There was usually a big ol' graniteware coffee pot sittin' towards the back, maybe a tea kettle, and sometimes a double boiler that would turn out a lip smackin' mug of hot chocolate to help warm stiff, cold little hands that a few minutes before had been pullin' on a sled rope. At butcherin' time, a big ol' pot sat there, rendering out the leaf lard for cookin' or the rest of the fat for soap. And when a potful was finished, the deep fried pork skins or "cracklin's" were heaped on a platter and salted to make a treat for young and old.

Many of the old stoves had a water reservoir that could dispense piping hot water for washing clothes or taking a bath. And that's where the fond memories get a little hard edged.

Every Saturday night Mother would ask Dad to bring in the big tin washtub. She'd pour hot water into it, leaving enough in the reservoir to bring the temperature up in the tub when it got too cool. She'd pour cold water into the tub until it was right for a bath and then start grabbin' kids. The girls went first; then the boys got sluiced around a while. When the kids were all bathed, then it was Mother's turn. When she finished, Dad got in. I say "got in" because I can't rightly call it "takin' a bath." I can't rightly say it, because, by that time, what was in that tub couldn't rightly be called water. I've seen those tubs emptied out and, brother, there were some tough folks runnin' around the country back then ... dirty, too. Still, it was how things were done in those days, and nobody gave it a second thought.

Remember the cupholder screwed to the wall over the sink? Or the cup out in the pumphouse? If there was an old pitcher pump outside, it probably had a cup or dipper tied to it with a string. We all drank out of the same glass or cup in those days, and I don't think we were any less healthy than we are now.

Well, those days are gone now, but sometimes, on a cold winter morning, I come in from outside and still expect to smell hot, wet leather and see a pair of boots drying out while they sit on the open oven door of the old wood range. And, just once more, I'd like to see those boots still occupied, their owner sitting tipped back in a scuffed wooden chair, with his feet propped on the oven door while he enjoys a steaming mug of coffee from the old granite pot.


By the way, if you wanted to make a bar of soap that would float in water, how would you go about it? Right. You'd mix enough air in with the soap before makin' it into bars that the stuff couldn't help but float ... and we're not exactly original thinkers on this subject.

This is a pretty healthy place to live. The country had been settled for years, but there was still one civic improvement lacking. They finally had to shoot a fella to start a graveyard. Now don't get the wrong idea. It's not like they committed murder. The guy was a lawyer, after all.

When you answer the phone and the first thing the caller says is, "Do you own your own home?" never admit that you do. That is, unless you're so hard up for somebody to talk to that you really enjoy hearing all about roofing, siding or insurance.

Pete says he's figured out a sure way to make money.

"All I've gotta do," he says, "is go do something really stupid. Not plain ol' every day garden variety stupid, but something a drooling idiot wouldn't consider due to the risks involved. Go climb some mountain peak in my Sunday-go-to-meetin's or paddle out to sea on an air mattress. It's best if I can find some other lunatic to go along. That way, when he almost drowns or freezes to death, or when he crawls into a grizzly's den and gives the critter a hotfoot ... I can haul his waterlogged, frozen or gnawed carcass back toward civilization. In the meantime, a thousand or so people stop what they're doing to go search for a couple of boneheads who had no business being out there in the first place. When they finally find us, camped on death's doorstep from freezing, drowning or bleeding, my partner will look up and say "Pete, you're a hero. You saved my life." Naturally, I'll act humble about the whole thing and then go write a magazine article or a book about it.

"I'm tellin' you," he says, "I'll make a fortune! By the way, any of you guys free this weekend?"


There's one thing you have to admit about kids. You've never had one whip out his wallet to show you snapshots of his dopey parents and then spend thirty minutes telling you about the cute things they do at work.


If you've got problems with slugs or snails in your garden, the commercial bait available in garden supply stores works really well. The problem is that every time you water or it happens to rain, the pellets dissolve and you have to put out more. Try cutting out both ends of a tall tin can and squash the sides down until they're only an inch or two apart. Put your bait in there and put it in your garden. It's sheltered from the water, but the slimy little critters can still get to it just fine.

The tougher the decision, the fewer the number of people who will be around to help you make it. But they'll be back just as soon as the results are in -- good or bad.

We were all sittin' around one morning not long ago gettin' coffeed up, as usual. Tom had been goin' on for quite a while about the problems he was havin' down at the store.

Finally, Joe settled back in his chair, took a sip of coffee, and stared out the window. "You know, Tom," he said quietly, "the only people who really like to hear about your troubles are your mother and your enemies."

Makes sense to me.

Horses, you know, are a lot like people. There are good ones, bad ones, smart ones, and dumb ones. And sometimes you run across one who just likes to aggravate folks out of the sheer joy of it. We had one like that when I was a kid. His name was Comet.

Now, you might think he was named Comet because he was so fast, and he was that alright, but I always thought it was due to the speed a rider built up when he came flyin' off him. Ol' Comet could flat out buck! He didn't do it out of meanness or because he was scared, you understand. He did it because he was young and strong and so full of spit and vinegar he just couldn't hardly stand it.

We started him out like all the other colts, teachin' him to lead and, later on, to take the bit and finally the saddle. He was over two years old when my brother finally got on him. Jim rode him around the corral a while, and Comet didn't seem to mind too much. After ten minutes or so, with things goin' so smooth and all, Jim asked me to open the gate so he could ride around the small pasture in back of the barn.

Now Comet was a big black with a blaze face and, even then, probably weighed close to a thousand pounds. He went along kind of jerky like a horse will do when he's bein' ridden for the first time. After about ten more minutes, Jim was telling me what a good horse this was gonna be and how this would be his personal mount from now on.

Well, maybe Jim relaxed too much, or maybe ol' Comet just decided he'd put up with this nonsense long enough, but anyhow he just up and exploded. I've gotta give Jim credit. He stayed with him for eight or ten jumps and, believe me, ol' Comet had talent. He could sunfish with the best of 'em and come down with four stiff legs, one after the other so you'd feel each jolt separately. He'd gotten some free

49

rein by that time, and he put his head down between his front legs and went to work. He could get higher than any horse I ever saw, and when he got up there, he was shakin' like a wet dog. The last jump was something special, and he launched ol' Jim so high, I thought that before he got back to earth, he'd probably freeze his ears off. Jim landed on his head. He was only out cold for twenty minutes or so, and I made myself useful in the meantime. I pried open his hands and took out about half a bushel of horsehair, picked some more of it out of his teeth, and then went and found his hat. When Dad found us, I was usin' it to slap off some of the dirt and horse manure he'd collected when he hit the ground. Dad had me help him pack Jim up to the house, but I couldn't see what all the excitement was about. I told him if Jim had landed anywhere but on his head, he could have hurt himself. Dad didn't see it that way.

Well, the next mornin' Jim was out tryin' ol' Comet again. The results were pretty much the same that day and every day. Finally, after a week or so, ol' Comet misjudged a little, I guess, because Jim landed on his side and broke his arm. While Mom hauled him to the doctor, Dad cut himself a hunk of harness leather and got on ol' Comet. It was quite a show.

Now, I'll admit Dad was chokin' the biscuit (that's grabbin' the saddle horn), but there's times when pullin' leather only makes sense, and this was one of 'em. Dad beat a tattoo on ol' Comet's rump

until that horse got the idea that maybe this wasn't quite so much fun after all. It made a good horse out of him, or at least as good as he was gonna get.

Comet was a good one alright. He was big and strong and fast, and he had good cow sense, too. But when you throwed a leg over ol' Comet, you'd better be ready. He gave up the buckin' business, but if you weren't payin' attention, he'd scrape you off on the first tree or fence post he could find. He'd pretend to shy at a scrap of paper or whatever and jump sideways about twenty feet. If he dumped you, then you could plan on walkin' home. You couldn't just tie him up, either. He'd keep pickin' at the knot until he got himself loose. There wasn't a gate on the place he couldn't open. We had to wire 'em shut.

Yep, when you got on ol' Comet you better be ready, because you were on a real horse. Of course, you had to catch him first, and that could be next to impossible. There was only one exception: you could walk out into the pasture with a gang of little kids and Comet would just stand there. You could walk right up to him and start throwin' kids on his back until they were lined up mane to tail, and he wouldn't turn a hair. The kids would be yellin' and laughin' and kickin' Comet in the flanks, and he'd mosey around like the tamest old plug on earth. But an adult? Be ready, brother.

By the time he was four, Comet would go about eleven hundred pounds and was at the top of the pecking order of the bunch. Every other horse gave way to him. He never gave up tryin' to get the best of his riders, either.

One of his tricks was to blow up (hold his breath) when you were cinchin' the saddle on him. If you weren't careful, you'd find yourself sittin' a saddle that didn't have a cinch touchin' ol' Comet's belly. The trick was to wait him out and make him breathe. Comet figured that one out, too. While you were waitin', your attention was likely to wander. Comet would stand there, swishin' his tail like the flies were botherin' him, shiftin' his feet around a little and just waitin'. When he knew you weren't alert, he'd just pick up his left front foot and put that iron shod hoof down on the toe of your boot ... and then lean on it. Of course, you'd find him right up against you, too close to really haul off and punch him, and all the time he'd be actin' like something happenin' somewhere on the horizon was just too fascinatin' to pay any attention to all that screamin' and cussin' goin' on right next to him. And, well, I don't know about you, but personally I've found havin' an eleven hundred pound horse standin' on my foot to be a sure cure for problems with irregularity. Yeah, horses are a lot like people. Some of 'em have real character. And some of 'em more than necessary.


Ever notice when joining a group of people you don't know that often the first person to act like a friend is doing it because he doesn't have one?

We were talkin' about children the other day, and Pete said "Well, once when the kids were young, I drove 'em into the city and took 'em to the zoo."

Silence.

Then more silence.

Finally, Luther says, "Yeah, so?"

"Oh," grumbled Pete, "after three or four days, Gladys got to missin' 'em and made me go get 'em back."


Anyone thinking of becoming a parent should cultivate a love of the great outdoors. This is because once you actually become a parent, you'll find so much of the outdoors winding up indoors.


"I don't get it," says Tom. "Some guy studies to be an idiot, can't make the grade, and instead becomes an actor. The next thing you know, he's on television or in the movies and everything changes. People follow him around, taking his picture and wanting his autograph. They ask his opinion on everything under the sun. Pretty soon this guy believes he's an authority on just about anything. All of a sudden there he is, doing a sixty second bit on television describing a social problem, defining what makes it a problem, and telling us what we have to do to fix it to his satisfaction. Well, if the guy had a conscience, he wouldn't be using his notoriety to try to influence me to think the way he does. And, besides, it goes against my grain to agree with anybody who has the IQ of an eggplant."

A lot of city folks are out there at the new golf course playin' cow pasture pool. Not a cow to be seen anywhere. Now if you want to talk about the bull, that's another story.

Golfers are good walkers, good criers and mighty poor adders.

Her name was Charity, and she had written a book called Lady Logger. I met her at the county fair where I was manning a booth for our local veterans group. The booth next to me was occupied by a dozen or so writers from around the state who were selling autographed copies of their books. Charity was sittin' at the end of the row, three feet from where I was handing out literature about and for the veterans.

I'd say Charity was about seventy at the time, tall and lean with a real aggressive attitude. I recall I talked with her for five minutes before I realized that she wasn't a man.

Well, anyhow, Charity it seemed, had spent forty years in the woods logging right along with the men.  There wasn't a thing she didn't know about the business and not a well-known person in the industry that she didn't know personally.  It was all right there in her book, and she meant for people to read it ... even if she had to reach out and grab 'em as they walked by.  And if they dared to say they didn't want the book, she got mad.  Well, she did sell some books alright, but sittin' next to her, I had trouble gettin' people to take my free pamphlets.

The toughest part though was  that Charity didn't seem to have a sense of humor.  I tried to joke with her from time to time, like telling her not to stay out too late that night so she could be at the booth on time the next day.  But every time I said something, she was right in my face saying, "I want you to know I'm a lady!  I've always been a lady!  The men I worked with knew that I was a lady, and you can bet I never allowed any of 'em to forget it!  Just because I was a logger didn't mean I wasn't a lady ... understand?"

Yep.

Funny, but as luck would have it, about six months later I happened to have cause to travel to the very area she was from.  Everybody I met in that little town had a story about Charity.  She'd had five or six husbands, some now dead, the others still in hiding and enough boyfriends to fill a good-sized stadium.  Out in the brush, folks said, she lived up to her name by being as charitable as possible to just about anybody who came along. She could outdance, outdrink, outcuss, outchew and outspit most of the men in the country, and I'm only mentioning her more charming qualities.

Well, I admit it. I was bamboozled. I should have remembered what my mother always said: "If a woman has to keep tellin' folks she's a lady ... she probably ain't."

I firmly believe that if you were to go down to the statehouse and talk to every elected official you can find, sooner or later you'll come across an innocent man.

Our oldest son, Kyle, began to notice girls when he was still pretty young. I mentioned it to Martha.

"Don't worry about it," she said. "It's just a stage he's going through. He'll get over it in about seventy years."

First you get to the lie. Then you arrive at the damned lie. From there, with the aid of a powerful telescope, you can see the lawyers.

Luther says he was out in his barn a while back when he spotted a bum cuttin' across his cow pasture. The bum was headed toward a freight train that was just pullin' out of a siding after lettin' an express go by. The problem was that Beauregard had spotted the bum, too.

Now you don't know Beauregard, but he's Luther's Holstein bull. Ol' Beauregard is probably an ax handle and a half between the eyes, has feet the size of turkey platters and is about as happy as you'd expect a fella to be who has thirty mothers-in-law. On his good days he drops back to plain ol' homicidal maniac.

"Anyhow," Luther says, "ol' Beauregard gets to blowin' snot an' steam an' pretty soon them big ol' feet are hittin' the ground and throwin' up chunks of sod big enough for these city fellers to make a fair-sized puttin' green. The bum spots him and the race is on. Halfway across the pasture a jackrabbit jumps out of the brush ahead of him, and the bum yells, *Move over rabbit and let somebody run who knows how!*"

"Did he make the train?" I asked.

"No," says Luther, with a shake of his head. "Overshot it completely. I heard later that he ran through the back of the caboose on that passenger train, and before he could stop himself, he was sittin' up with the first class passengers and owed the railroad eighteen dollars.

That same old story is making the rounds again. Every once in a while somebody comes up with the idea that people on welfare should work for what they get and wants a law passed to that effect. It'll never happen. How would a bill like that ever get through Congress? They'd think it applied to themselves.

I had a dog once who could say his own name. He was just an old potlicker and not good for much, but sometimes I miss ol' Ralph.

We had a fella in here last Veterans' Day complaining about all the undue attention and consideration given to veterans.

"I don't think it's right," he was sayin'. "Rather than be drafted and sent to Vietnam, I stood up for my principles. I went to Canada. You can bet that if it had been a morally correct war, I would have gone. I might even have enlisted, in fact. World War Two, now I would have fought in that one."

You can tell when Tom is really peeved, because his forehead wrinkles while one eyebrow raises about an inch. "You know," he said, and took a sip of coffee, "I've got a willow switch down at the store that I use for huntin' sabertoothed tigers. If there was just one around, I'd show you how I do it."

I can't tell you exactly what Pete said, but it

was a one word statement concerning fertilizer and male cattle. The fella glanced at Pete and then turned on his stool to look at me, expecting support, I guess.

"Don't look at me," I said. "I'm a veteran myself, and if you don't understand by now, then nobody could explain it to you so that you would."

You could tell that he thought otherwise, but I'd told him the truth. Which is more than we thought he'd done for us.


We used to go through light bulbs right and left around here. Then I found out our voltage was a little higher than normal. A lot of electrical and lighting stores carry the higher capacity 130 volt light bulbs. They don't cost any more and last a whole lot longer. If you're burning out bulbs faster than you think is normal, you might want to give 'em a try.


"Now, that country down south," says Luther, "is high, dry, flat and covered in sagebrush. You can see more of it with one look than just about anyplace else. It's tough on horses, tougher on people, and you don't ever want to buy a huntin' rifle that's been used in that country. Folks tend to shoot at ranges that are just way too long," he nods. "Strains the gun."

"You know," says Tom, "I've got a sporting goods section in my hardware store, and I've come to the conclusion that, for some reason, fishermen and golfers are notably poor at math."

With some guys, the longer and louder they argue, the better the chance that they're wrong -- and know it.

Okay, maybe I'm not the most regular church-goer in town, but I do try to get there every so often. If I'm bein' checked off on a tally book somewhere, I want to improve my chances of relaxing in heaven rather than freezing in hell. Yep. You see, I've been thinkin' about it, and what with all the politicians, used car salesmen, lawyers, and news reporters, I don't see how I'd ever get close enough to the fire to get warm.

I know you've gotta be on your way, but I see you've still got a swallow of coffee left, so hold up your cup. A toast before you leave:
May you always be happy ... and may your enemies know it.